The
Asian Tsunami
2004

A huge wave kills thousands

JOHN TOWNSEND

www.raintreepublishers.co.uk

Visit our website to find out more information about **Raintree** books.

To order:

☎ Phone 44 (0) 1865 888113

📄 Send a fax to 44 (0) 1865 314091

💻 Visit the Raintree bookshop at **www.raintreepublishers.co.uk** to browse our catalogue and order online.

First published in Great Britain by Raintree, Halley Court, Jordan Hill, Oxford OX2 8EJ, part of Harcourt Education.
Raintree is a registered trademark of Harcourt Education Ltd.

Editorial: Andrew Farrow and Richard Woodham
Design: Victoria Bevan and AMR Design Ltd
Illustrations: David Woodroffe
Picture Research: Maria Joannou and
   Ginny Stroud-Lewis
Production: Helen McCreath

Originated by Modern Age
Printed and bound in China by South China
   Printing Company

13 digit ISBN 978 1 406 20291 5 (hardback)
10 09 08 07 06
10 9 8 7 6 5 4 3 2 1

13 digit ISBN 978 1 406 20301 1 (paperback)
11 10 09 08 07
10 9 8 7 6 5 4 3 2 1

British Library Cataloguing in Publication Data
Townsend, John
The Asian Tsunami, 2004. - (When disaster
   struck)
363.3'494'091824
A full catalogue record for this book is available
from the British Library.

Acknowledgements
The publishers would like to thank the following for permission to reproduce photographs:

Alamy Images p. 11 (Leisa Hale); Corbis pp. 9 (NEWS LTD/AUSTRAL), 20 (Babu/Reuters), 40); Empics pp. 4 (AP/APTN), 16 (AP/APTN), 19 (AP/Vincent Thian), 24 (AP/Huang Wen Feng, Chief Officer MV Durban Bridge), 25 (AP), 29 (AP/MANISH SWARUP), 35 (AP/WONG MAYE-E), 42 (Bart A Bauer/USN/Abaca/ABACA), 43 (AP/APTN); Getty Images pp. 12 (AFP), 13, 22), 34, 38, 41, 44, 48 (Photodisc); NASA p. 18 (GSFC/Jacques Descloitres, MODIS Land Rapid Response Team); Nature Picture Library p. 47; Rex Features pp. 10 (Eye Ubiquitous), 14 (Digital Globe), 14 (Digital Globe), 33 (Sipa Press), 36 (Sipa Press), 46 (DCY), 49 (Masatoshi Okauchi), Steve Hunter pp. 26, 27); Topham Picturepoint pp. 28 (Zorah/The Image Works), 30 (US Navy/Photographer's Mate 3rd Class Rebecca J. Moat), 32 (Photri/US Navy/Photographer's mate 2nd Class Dennis Cantrell), 37 (US Navy/Photographer's Mate 3rd Class Jacob J. Kirk).

Cover photograph of the tsunami, reproduced with permission of Empics (Eric Skitzi/AP).

The publishers would like to thank Mike Freeman of Samaritan's Purse for his assistance in the preparation of this book. Samaritan's Purse works to meet the critical needs of victims of war, poverty, famine, disease, and natural disaster.

CONTENTS

551·2   R414495

Any words appearing in the text in bold, **like this**, are explained in the glossary.

A HUGE WAVE KILLS THOUSANDS

The Asian Tsunami, 2004

FAR BELOW THE SEA

Just before 8:00 a.m. local time on 26 December 2004, the ground shook near Sumatra in Indonesia.

About 240 kilometres (150 miles) off the coast of Sumatra and about 30 kilometres (19 miles) below the ocean floor, an earthquake jolted the seabed for nearly 10 minutes. It was one of the most powerful earthquakes ever recorded.

The quake churned up the sea and sent the deadliest waves on record sweeping across the Indian Ocean. Waves reached speeds of 480 kilometres (300 miles) per hour. Waves measuring between 4 and 15 metres high crashed on to beaches in Indonesia, Thailand, Sri Lanka, and India. Waves even reached Africa, 4,800 kilometres (3,000 miles) away.

A British tourist's video footage shows the huge wave hitting Phuket, Thailand.

WHEN THE WAVE STRUCK

The Asian Tsunami, 2004

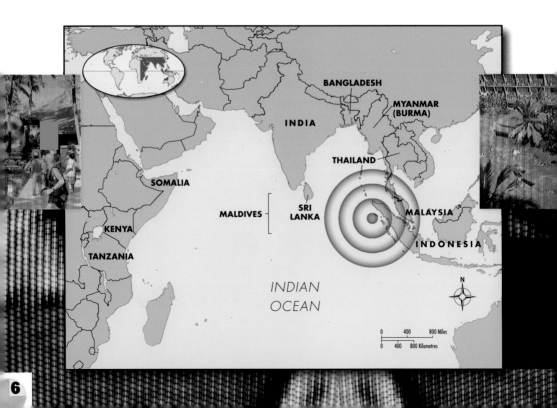

BANGLADESH

INDIA

MYANMAR (BURMA)

THAILAND

SOMALIA

MALDIVES

SRI LANKA

MALAYSIA

KENYA

INDONESIA

TANZANIA

INDIAN OCEAN

N

| 0 | 400 | 800 Miles |
| 0 | 400 | 800 Kilometres |

JUST ANOTHER DAY

The morning started as usual for millions of people in countries and islands all around the Indian Ocean.

For many people in Indonesia, that meant farming or fishing near the villages where their families had lived for generations. Traders set out their market stalls in the streets of busy coastal towns. In many **remote** villages along the coast, people lived simply and owned very little. Some people made pots or handmade crafts to sell to tourists.

On the west coast of Thailand, the beach resorts were full with Christmas holiday-makers. Tourists were swimming, sunbathing, or eating breakfast beneath the palm trees. At 7:59 a.m., scientists at the Pacific Tsunami Warning Centre detected a major earthquake in the Indian Ocean. They still had no idea it had triggered a deadly wave.

This map shows where the earthquake took place, and the countries affected by the resulting waves.

WHAT WAS KNOWN?

Tsunami is a Japanese word meaning "harbour wave". People living near the sea in many parts of the world have always known about the dangers of tsunamis. Throughout history, tsunamis have struck coasts around parts of the Indian and Pacific Oceans. They can happen when the Earth's **crust** breaks or moves under the sea. This movement causes giant waves to spread out like huge ripples. The waves can be many metres high and travel huge distances.

Earthquakes often occur near Indonesia, in the Indian Ocean. Here, huge pieces of the Earth's crust called **plates** push against each other. Sometimes they move suddenly and cause the Earth to shake. Whenever this happens under the sea, a tsunami can form.

THE WORLD'S WORST TSUNAMIS 1994–2003

Date	Place	Reason	Deaths
3 June 1994	Java, Indonesia	Earthquake	223
17 February 1996	Biak, Irian Java	Earthquake	166
21 February 1996	Peru	Earthquake	7
17 November 1996	Near Brownsville, Texas	Bad weather	10
17 July 1998	Papua New Guinea	Earthquake	2,000+
15 September 1999	Marquesas Islands	Landslide	0

Earthquakes can range from small tremors to massive quakes. Scientists measure the strength of an earthquake and give it a number from 1 to 9 on the **Richter scale**. The earthquake on 26 December 2004 measured 9 on the Richter scale. Scientists knew an enormous earthquake had struck. They could only wait to learn what damage it would cause.

The village of Sissano was destroyed in July 1998 when a tsunami hit Papua New Guinea.

THE FIRST SIGNS

From the beaches of Thailand, the sea looked calm beneath the warm morning sun. People could hear the waves breaking gently on the shore. That was until flocks of birds began chirping noisily in the trees. Monkeys screeched and ran into the higher branches. A few people heard dolphins making strange noises just offshore.

On Khao Lak beach in Thailand, the elephants were at work as usual, giving rides to tourists. Suddenly they made loud, wailing cries and stomped the ground. Those still tied to posts broke their chains and ran. Their owners could not calm them or stop them from running up into the hills, taking their tourist riders with them.

Minutes later a loud roaring sound came from the beach. The people on high ground could only watch as a wall of water smashed across the sand and swept people away.

DID YOU KNOW?

Elephants have often been known to sense disaster before it strikes. Scientists believe that they can sense small vibrations with their feet and trunk. Perhaps they sensed the earthquake and knew danger was coming?

Elephant rides are popular with tourists in Thailand.

The beautiful coastline of Khao Lak National Park in Thailand was badly damaged by the tsunami.

People at sea were the first to know something was wrong. Some of the fishermen just thought there was a very high tide. The water level seemed far higher than usual for that time of day. Others thought a storm was coming as the sea suddenly became quite rough. But others had very little time to think at all. The force of the wave **capsized** many boats, and smashed others on to beaches. Few people had any idea of what was really happening.

First, the tsunami struck the island of Sumatra, in Indonesia. It was just before 8:30 a.m. local time (1:30 a.m. **GMT**), less than 30 minutes after the ground had stopped shaking. A 15-metre-high wave smashed on to beaches. It threw boats on to houses and tore trees from the sides of hills that were 800 metres (2,600 feet) inland. People had no warning and did not know what was happening. They had no idea that they were the first victims in the tsunami's path.

ON THE BEACHES

From many beaches, the first sign of the approaching waves was a line of white foam on the **horizon**. At first it seemed nothing to worry about. Swimmers stood and watched. Fishermen stared from their boats. The waves came nearer and grew larger. In places they were more than 20 metres (65 feet) high. Some people began to scream and run. There was chaos as parents tried to gather their children.

On this beach in Thailand, Karin Svaerd ran towards the waves to help her family escape. Miraculously, the family all survived.

In other places, the first sign of anything unusual was the sea appearing to be sucked away, leaving fish stranded on the sand where the water had been. Boats raced for the shore at full speed. People on the beaches turned and ran. Soon, the huge wall of water smashed down on anything in its path.

The water rushed up the beaches, crashed into buildings, and poured through streets. The force of the waves destroyed anything in their way.

Many people did not realise how powerful the waves were until it was too late.

26 DECEMBER TIMELINE

7:59 a.m. local time
(12:59 a.m. GMT)
Huge earthquake off the coast of Sumatra

8:30 a.m. local time
(1:30 a.m. GMT)
Huge waves crash into Sumatra

9:30 a.m. local time
(2:30 a.m. GMT)
Waves hit beaches in southern Thailand

9:00 a.m. local time
(3:00 a.m. GMT)
Tsunami reaches Sri Lanka and the coast of India

9:30 a.m. local time
(4:30 a.m. GMT)
Tsunami hits the Maldives

10:00 a.m. local time
(7:00 a.m. GMT)
Tsunami strikes East Africa

THE FIRST CASUALTIES

The Asian Tsunami, 2004

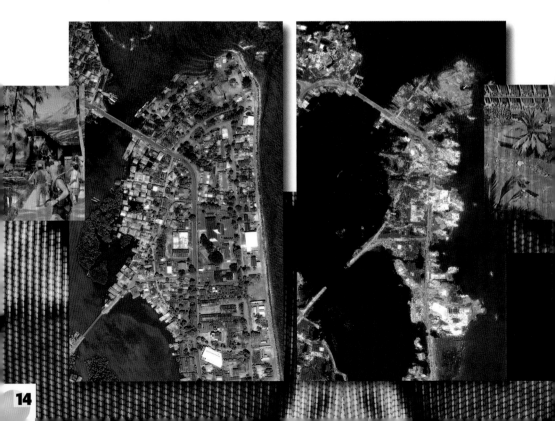

THE DAMAGE IN INDONESIA

Thousands of people died when the waves hit Sumatra.

The exact number of victims who were drowned or crushed to death by the waves will never be known. Many were washed out to sea. Six months after the disaster, bodies and skeletons were still being found.

About 500,000 Indonesian people were made homeless by the tsunami. They could only shelter in scattered camps and had to rely on **aid**. Relief organizations said it would take two years to get everyone rehoused.

The Indonesian city of Banda Aceh was one of the worst hit places. This coastal city was almost totally destroyed, killing thousands of people in just a few minutes.

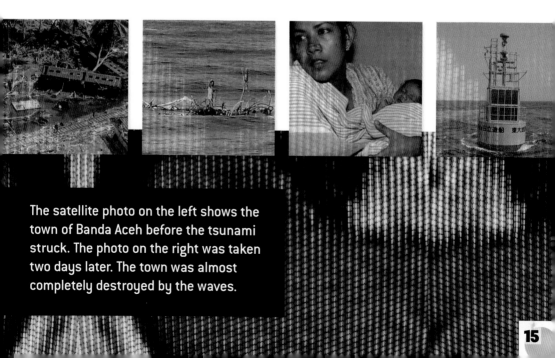

The satellite photo on the left shows the town of Banda Aceh before the tsunami struck. The photo on the right was taken two days later. The town was almost completely destroyed by the waves.

THE WAVES REACH THAILAND

Thousands of tourists travel to Thailand every year to enjoy the sun, sea, and golden sand. On 26 December 2004, many people were getting up late after Christmas parties the night before. But there were already many swimmers, divers, and sunbathers on the beaches at the resort of Phuket.

Soon after 9:30 a.m. local time, the sea suddenly seemed to change. People described it as moving strangely. A few swimmers screamed as they were sucked out to sea. In the hotels along the beach, people went out on to the balconies to see what was happening. Others rushed to the shoreline. As in Indonesia, it appeared as if the tide had suddenly gone out. Fish lay flapping on the damp sand and already people were picking them up. Rocks in the bay that usually poked just above the water were now towering above the sand.

Hotels along the coast were swamped by the sea.

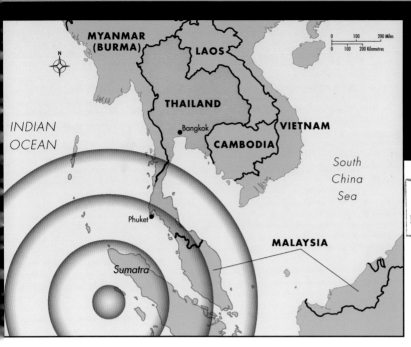

While everyone wondered what was happening, the sea began to rush back with a roar. The sea surged back at a frightening speed. It crashed up the beach and smashed into the hotels. It washed away chairs and tables from the shore, lifted cars off the road, and hurled them into buildings. It gushed into hotel lobbies, filling rooms with water and **debris**. It poured into basements, swirled up stairways, and broke down doors.

More waves followed, smashing through the streets and knocking down people. Hundreds of shop windows broke as the **torrent** of water burst through them. Now armed with broken glass, the water ripped at people's bodies as they tried to cling to anything they could find.

"YOU KEEP RUNNING"

"What do you do when you see a huge wave-wall coming at you? You run. You run as fast as you can. You think, 'This isn't real.' But you keep running [...] until the water lifts you off your feet and sweeps you onwards.
It makes no difference whether you can swim or not. The force carries you forward. Grab on to something and you may live. Surf the wave and you have a chance. Hit something solid, and you die."

Les Boardman, 56, an Australian who was on the beach at Phuket, Thailand

THE WAVES REACH SRI LANKA

Apart from Indonesia, Sri Lanka suffered more casualties from the tsunami than anywhere else. Its southern coast was torn apart. Crops and fishing boats were flattened and wrecked. More than 100,000 homes were damaged or destroyed, and more than 500,000 people were made homeless.

The tsunami led to one of the worst rail disasters in the world. At Telwatta, in the southwest of Sri Lanka, a train was knocked sideways when the tsunami hit. Up to 1,500 people were crammed inside the train as it travelled from Colombo to Galle.

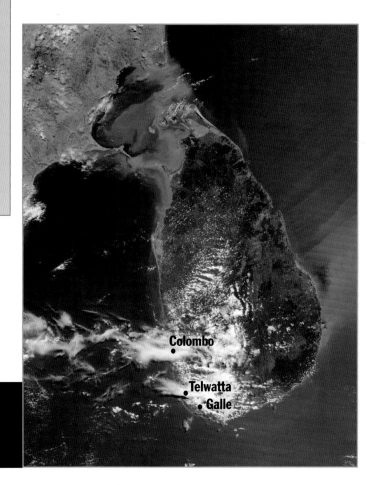

Coastal areas in the south of Sri Lanka were hit by the waves.

The force of the waves threw the train's eight cars far from the rails.

ESTIMATED 1,000 DEAD ON SRI LANKAN TRAIN

"Police estimated that around 1,000 people were killed when their train, the *Queen of the Sea*, was thrown off the track by this week's raging tsunami. Hundreds of bodies that were pulled from the twisted wreckage were buried Tuesday alongside the railway line.

The train had come to a stop amid rising waters just before it was struck by the giant wave. Many of the dead were villagers living nearby who tried to escape the waves by climbing on to the top of the train. The force of the waves tore off some of the wheels, and the tracks twisted like a loop on a roller coaster."

The Associated Press, 29 December 2004

THE DAMAGE IN INDIA AND THE MALDIVES

The giant waves spread across the Indian Ocean. Two hours after the earthquake, they reached India. Yet again, people on the beaches were swept away.

The tsunami swamped the roads at this beach in southern India.

The southeast coast of India was the worst hit, with the sea reaching 3 kilometres (2 miles) inland in places. More than 150,000 homes were destroyed, and over 600 kilometres (370 miles) of roads and 14 bridges were damaged. The muddy salt water **contaminated** fresh water supplies. Farmland and crops were ruined. Jetties used for getting supplies to the many islands were smashed apart.

The tsunami continued to rush across the Indian Ocean. At 9:30 a.m. local time (4:30 a.m. GMT), it struck the low-lying Maldive Islands. Of the 199 islands, 20 were described as "totally destroyed". Over 4,000 homes were destroyed and about 100 people were killed.

By now, the news of the tsunami was being sent around the world. Very few details were known but there was enough time to warn countries still in the wave's path. It was heading towards Africa and it became a race against time to warn people. Some people heard the news and rushed inland but not everyone received the warning in time.

Between 10:00 and 11.00 a.m. local time (7:00 and 8:00 a.m. GMT), the tsunami hit the coasts of Somalia and Kenya in eastern Africa. It had taken 6–7 hours for the waves to travel 4,800 kilometres (3,000 miles) across the Indian Ocean. In May 2005 the Red Cross reported that the tsunami killed 312 people in East Africa (Kenya, Madagascar, Seychelles, Somalia, and Tanzania).

THE CASUALTIES

Indonesia:
130,000 dead
37,000 missing

Thailand:
5,395 dead
2,800 missing

Sri Lanka:
31,000 dead
4,000 missing

India:
11,000 dead

Casualties were also reported in the Maldives, Malaysia, Burma, Bangladesh, Somalia, Kenya, Tanzania, and the Seychelles.

THE LUCKY
SURVIVORS

The Asian Tsunami, 2004

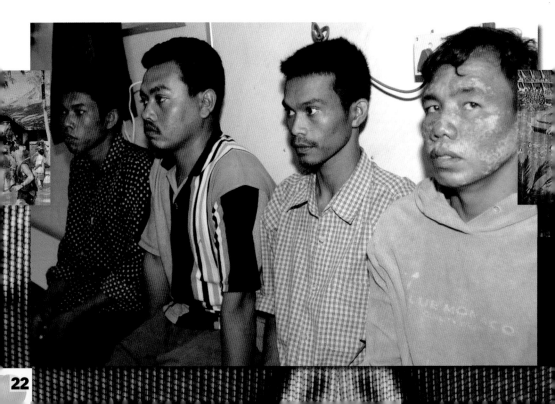

AMAZING ESCAPES

News of the disaster spread quickly around the world.

However, it took days before the world knew the full scale of what had happened. No one had realised how many people had been killed, injured, or left homeless. When survivors told of what happened, the world was stunned. Newspapers were full of survivors' stories. Some were about people who just happened to be in the right place at the right time and escaped being washed away. Others were about people who ran to safety, like the 10-year-old British girl who remembered her geography lesson about tsunamis. When she saw the water disappearing from a beach in Thailand, she told her family to run away just before the waves came back.

There were amazing stories of fishermen surviving at sea for days in smashed boats. Among all the tragic stories, there were amazing accounts of survival.

These four fishermen from Sumatra were rescued by helicopter after the tsunami smashed their boat. They drifted for nine days in a dinghy with no food or water.

DAYS AT SEA

No one will ever know how many thousands of people were dragged out to sea by the retreating waves. The chances of anyone surviving long in the Indian Ocean were low. Yet there were some amazing stories about survivors.

Rizal Shahputra was 23 and cleaning a **mosque** in Aceh province, Sumatra, when the tsunami hit. "Everybody sank; my family sank. There were bodies around me," he said. He grabbed on to an uprooted palm tree and was swept out to sea. He clung on for 8 days as currents took him 160 kilometres (100 miles) out into the ocean. He kept alive by drinking rainwater and eating coconuts from the palm tree. At last he saw a ship in the distance and waved to it. One of the crew saw Rizal and the ship picked him up. He was taken to a hospital in Malaysia. Amazingly, Rizal only had minor injuries.

Spotted by sailors on a Japanese ship, Rizal Shahputra was taken to neighbouring Malaysia.

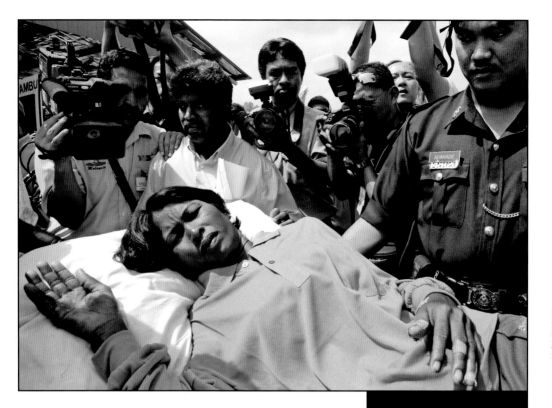

Another 23-year-old from Aceh had a lucky escape. Her name was Melawati and she, too, was swept out to sea where she was adrift for days.

Melawati had seen sharks circling her raft while she was adrift.

WOMAN SAVED FROM WAVES

"A Malaysian tuna ship rescued a woman who had drifted for five days in the Indian Ocean. Last week's tsunami swept her out to sea from her home on Sumatra island.

Melawati was spotted alive and clinging to an uprooted palm tree. She had leg injuries as a result of being bitten by fish. She was very weak as her only food had been the palm tree's fruit and bark. Crew members aboard a trawler saw Melawati in her badly torn clothes, waving at them. They helped her climb aboard and took her to a hospital on Malaysia's Penang island. The crew said Melawati cried throughout her three days aboard the trawler."

The Sydney Morning Herald

STEVE HUNTER'S STORY

Steve Hunter from the United Kingdom was working as a deep-sea diver on Phi Phi Island off the coast of Thailand. He was still in bed when the tsunami struck. The story of what happens begins in the panel below.

"IT SOUNDED LIKE THUNDER"

"It was the noise that woke me. It sounded like thunder and falling water. I ran to the window to look outside. Down in the street I could see water. It was just a trickle at first – crawling through the dust. Just then a crack ripped through the door with a loud splintering of wood. The door burst open as if it had been kicked in. Water crashed into the room and pinned me against the wall. I could only gasp for breath before the wall fell down all around me and I blacked out.

When I woke, I was treading water but I had no idea where I was. It was dark and my head was banging on a concrete ceiling. The water was rising even higher. I sucked in some air and dived down to a hole between jagged bricks. Suddenly I was carried along in a gush of water and found myself outside. There was blood and a huge gash at my ankle. It looked as if a sheet of iron from the roof had sliced through my leg. I didn't think I was going to survive."

Steve Hunter was incredibly lucky to survive the disaster.

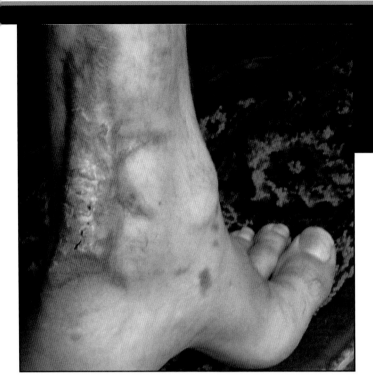

Steve Hunter's leg took many months to heal. This picture was taken 9 months after the disaster.

Steve pulled himself up a hillside to get above the swirling water. He scrambled into a hut where other shocked people were sheltering. Someone looked at his ripped ankle and poured alcohol on it to kill any germs from the dirty water. He screamed in pain and lay awake all night, hoping for help to arrive. The next day some men carried Steve outside and at last a helicopter rushed him to hospital. His ankle was badly wounded and he had lost a lot of blood.

After surgery, he was flown to Bangkok Hospital for further treatment. It took over a year and many operations before Steve could walk properly again. But he had been lucky. The night before the tsunami struck, he had been staying in a hut on the beach. The wave washed away the hut and all the people staying there. "I'm so lucky to be alive," he said. "My friends were killed but I survived."

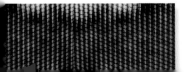

UNDER THE RUBBLE

Can you imagine being buried alive for two weeks? A 60-year-old man called Sirasena was found under the rubble of Galle in Sri Lanka. He was only able to mumble his name and that he had a son and daughter. Sirasena was very weak and had a broken arm. By the state of his body, doctors could tell he had been under the rubble for almost two weeks. He probably stayed alive by drinking rainwater.

A month after the disaster, there seemed to be no chance of any more missing people being found. But then came more good news. A police party found five men, three children, and one woman in a remote part of Campbell Bay, an island in the Indian Ocean. They had been there for 38 days. The weak survivors said they had been swept into the sea by the wave and were later thrown back on to the beach. They survived by eating coconuts and kept hoping someone would find them. Their hope paid off.

Many people were buried under rubble when houses and other buildings collapsed.

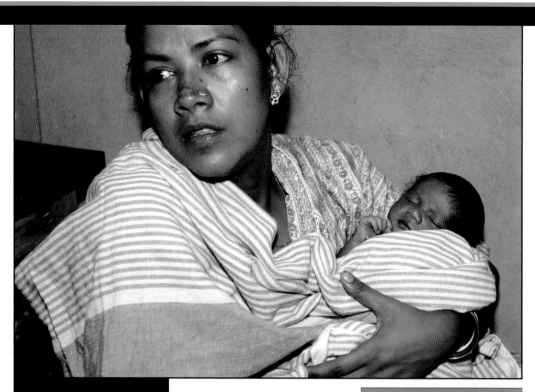

Tsunami was born just a few hours after the waves struck.

Hours after fleeing her home on an island in the Indian Ocean, Namita Roy gave birth on a jungle hilltop. She and her husband had to wait there with 700 other survivors. They ate bananas and drank coconut milk for days before help arrived. Both mother and baby survived. The baby's name will always remind them of their survival story. He was called Tsunami.

People from over 50 countries were killed by the tsunami. These included over 250 people from Australia, over 150 from the UK, and over 50 from the USA. But many tourists had lucky escapes.

▶ A LUCKY ESCAPE

"We were out at sea in an 8-metre-long boat which was going from Thailand to a small island when we saw the tsunami. We were about 1 kilometre (half a mile) from shore when the boat driver very quickly headed for a nearby bay. We had enough time to plan for when we hit the beach. It was a very close call and we made it to shore with only about 10 seconds to spare. We ran to higher ground. We are thankful to say we have nothing more to show for it than just a few scratches."

Jason and Lisa Bagby, email to CNN

THE
WORLD
RESPONDS

The Asian Tsunami, 2004

TO THE RESCUE

As more and more news reached the world's television screens, people began to realise the scale of the disaster.

Hundreds of thousands of people needed help immediately. They needed food, clean water, blankets, shelter, and medical supplies. They needed workers to organise and deliver these supplies, and to look after all the casualties. The **United Nations** described this as the largest aid operation in the history of the world.

Relief organizations got to work straight away. Ships and planes full of materials for setting up camps were sent to the countries hit by the tsunami. Even with such a fast response, it took days before supplies reached some of the remote places. The waves had washed away many roads and bridges. Some villages could only be reached by helicopter.

Helicopters were used to bring emergency food and water supplies to survivors in hard-to-reach places.

A RACE AGAINST TIME

One of the first tasks was to recover the dead bodies. It was impossible to identify them all before they had to be buried. Even 2 months later, 500 bodies were still being found each day in Indonesia.

The risk of disease was a real problem. With the water supply contaminated, there was a danger that weak survivors could become ill. It was feared that **cholera** could cause more deaths than the tsunami itself.

Mosquitoes soon came to breed in the many large areas of **stagnant** water left after the floods. Mosquitoes spread **malaria**. Relief teams had to work fast to drain flooded areas and to bring in tanks of fresh water.

PEOPLE'S RESPONSES

People from all over the world were shocked by the scenes of devastation shown on television. They responded with gifts and fund-raising events. People and organizations raised over US $400 million in just a few days.

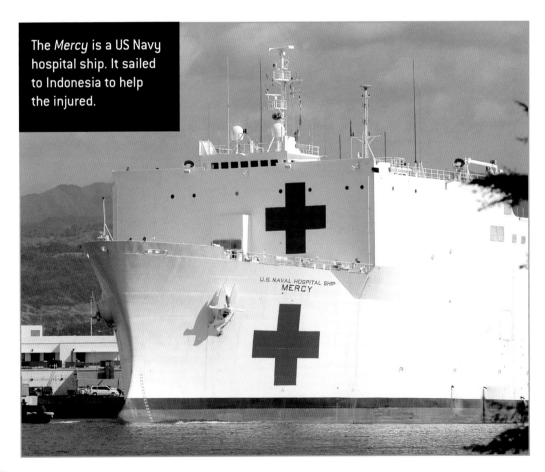

The *Mercy* is a US Navy hospital ship. It sailed to Indonesia to help the injured.

U.S. NAVAL HOSPITAL SHIP
MERCY

Trained dogs and elephants were used in some search-and-rescue operations. Dogs were used to detect dead bodies under piles of debris or in waterlogged areas. Elephants then lifted away heavy pieces of wood or concrete so that rescuers could retrieve the bodies.

A huge problem was tending to all the wounded. People with serious injuries were taken by helicopter to the crowded city hospitals. But many people living in the camps had scratches that became infected. Medical teams had to work fast to treat these infections.

Around 150 small camps sprung up within a week in Aceh, Sumatra. Relief workers encouraged all healthy people to work together to clear the debris. "The damage is mind-boggling, but they are rebuilding and everybody is moving around with a purpose," one of the doctors reported.

Camps set up for homeless people are often called refugee camps. The word "refugee" usually refers to someone who seeks shelter or a home for some reason. When reading about disasters you might come across the term "IDS" instead. IDS stands for "Internally Displaced Persons".

WITHIN WEEKS

Countries around the world promised to send money, workers, and equipment to rebuild areas hit by the tsunami. Governments from 87 countries gave over US $5 billion in total.

FEBRUARY 2005

Leaders from around the world visited the disaster areas. They saw for themselves what needed doing and helped to arrange more relief efforts. Two former US presidents toured camps and encouraged Americans to give more money. Bill Clinton and George Bush Senior spoke to the world about what they saw.

The Australian public raised over US $220 million and the government sent over US $1 billion. Australia also sent ships and aeroplanes to help.

People in Britain began giving money at the rate of £1 million an hour. After just a few weeks the public had raised £350 million (US $620 million). The British government sent £75 million (US $130 million) to help the rescue effort, as well as ships and helicopters.

Ships from the United States arrived in the disaster zones carrying supplies, thousands of troops, and about 50 helicopters. Other ships arrived that could turn sea water into clean drinking water. The United States also sent US $2 billion for relief work.

Former US presidents George H.W. Bush and Bill Clinton helped to raise money for the relief effort.

Giving money was one thing, but making sure it got to the right places was a difficult task. The first question facing everyone was where to start? It was vital for rescue teams to make an impact quickly. If survivors did not see help arriving soon, they would lose all hope. During the first few weeks after the tsunami, rescue work included providing emotional support as well as food, water, and medicine.

Doctors in the Singapore Army performed medical checks in temporary clinics in Sumatra.

Singapore was close to the **epicentre** of the earthquake on 26 December. However, it was sheltered from the tsunami by the island of Sumatra. Being close to the devastation of Sumatra, Singapore was able to get large rescue ships to the scene very quickly. The Singapore Armed Forces (SAF) organised its biggest-ever rescue, named Operation Flying Eagle. The SAF field hospitals in Meulaboh and Banda Aceh treated over 5,000 patients. Warships carried 190 tonnes of relief supplies, and SAF helicopters transported relief supplies and thousands of rescued people.

MONTHS LATER

Months after the tsunami struck, thousands of people were still living in camps. Some people had to sleep in the corridors of public buildings or anywhere they could find that gave shelter from rain.

There was **criticism** that the relief work took so long. But the scale and difficulty of the rebuilding needed a huge effort. No operation had been done on such a large scale before.

Many camps were still overcrowded six months after the disaster.

The Grand Mosque was one of the few buildings in Banda Aceh to remain standing after the waves hit.

All the planning and shipping of building materials, bulldozers, and cranes took a long time. The tsunami had also killed many skilled workers, so people had to be trained as builders.

Only when all the debris had been searched and cleared could the job of rebuilding begin. Slowly, the shattered villages, towns, roads, pipes, and cables are being put back together. The work will take many years to finish.

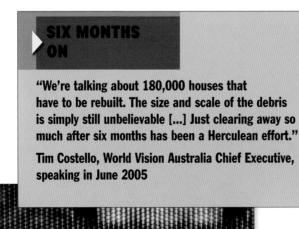

SIX MONTHS ON

"We're talking about 180,000 houses that have to be rebuilt. The size and scale of the debris is simply still unbelievable [...] Just clearing away so much after six months has been a Herculean effort."

Tim Costello, World Vision Australia Chief Executive, speaking in June 2005

CHILDREN OF THE TSUNAMI

The Asian Tsunami, 2004

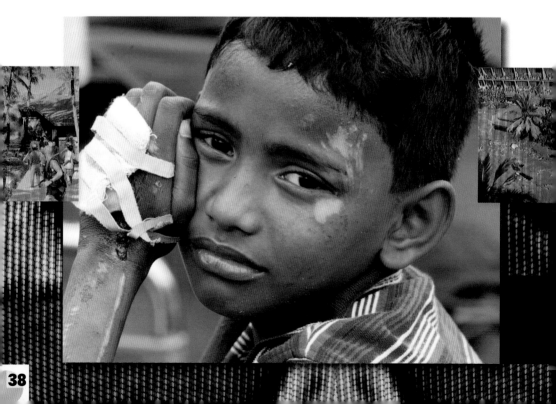

A DISASTER OF THE YOUNG

When disaster struck in the Indian Ocean in December 2004, millions of lives would never be the same again.

The tsunami changed the lives of many children forever. Thousands of children lost their families and their homes. Many were badly injured. It is estimated that 40 per cent of the dead were young children and babies. They were less able to run away, swim, or climb trees. They were also victims of disease in the days that followed. Even so, many children did manage to climb palm trees or run to higher ground. Some babies were found alive, floating on mattresses from their beds.

Despite all the survival stories, it was thought the tsunami left about 1.5 million children homeless. Many of the children were left **orphaned**.

The tsunami orphaned 35,000 children in Aceh province alone.

ORPHANS OF THE WAVES

The charity Save the Children organized toys, clothes, and medical supplies for the 35 children at this orphanage in Sri Lanka.

Once the waves had retreated, people were left confused, lost, and stunned. Children wandered through the rubble, trying to find anyone they knew. Some were lucky and found their family, but many others did not. It took months for relief workers to help children and their parents find each other. They had to find homes for the many orphans who had nowhere to go.

Children affected by the tsunami needed more than just shelter, medicine, and food. The **trauma** they had suffered left many young people in need of **counselling**. Children's charities tried to give emotional support to all those suffering from loss, grief, stress, and fear. It was important to help children feel secure again. Charities helped them get back to school. There they could play, learn, and talk about what had happened.

Although many schools had been washed away or used as shelters for the homeless, new schools were set up again. Some children will need help and support for many years.

TSUNAMI ORPHANS FLY HIGH!

Exactly 3 months after the tsunami struck, 27 orphaned children were given the ride of their lives. The Indian Air Force took each child for a flight in a microlight aircraft. The first child to go up was Reshmita. As she flew off in the plane, the other children on the ground waved and cheered. When she landed she giggled, "I am going to be a pilot!"

Helpers organized games such as volleyball to help children overcome the trauma they had suffered.

FOUND

Among all the tragic stories of parents or children being lost forever, there were some stories with happy endings.

After over six months apart, a father and daughter found each other again. Just before the tsunami struck, Muhamed Ali's 16-year-old daughter, Handayani, went to visit an aunt in the coastal town of Meulaboh, Sumatra. When the tsunami struck, Handayani disappeared and her father did not know if she was still alive. He moved to a camp after his wife and house were washed away. As time went by, there was no word of his missing daughter and he feared the worst.

US landing craft vehicles delivered supplies to the people of Meulaboh, on the island of Sumatra. The vehicles can transport more supplies than helicopters in a single trip.

In fact, she had survived and been taken to another camp. Several months later, government workers asked about Handayani's family. They traced her father and arranged to take her to him. When they met up again, they could not believe their eyes. "I thought she was dead," Muhamed Ali said. "This is amazing!"

BOY IS REUNITED WITH FATHER IN THAILAND

A weeping father found his missing 2-year-old son, Hannes, days after the tsunami. The family was on holiday from Sweden when the disaster struck. Someone found the small boy sitting alone on a roadside and took him to a hospital. Staff at the hospital posted his photo on the Internet to try to find his family. His uncle happened to see the photo and rushed to claim Hannes, whose father was in another hospital. At last father and son were brought together again. "I couldn't survive if I lost them both," the man said, telling how his wife had been dragged away by the wave.

The Internet helped to reunite this father with his son.

THE COST OF THE DISASTER

The Asian Tsunami, 2004

HOW MUCH?

Each of the countries affected by the disaster is still spending millions of dollars on repairing and rebuilding many areas.

There are many other costs, too. No one can tell how much the countries affected will lose in trade, crops, jobs, and tourists in the future. Some of the beaches, resorts, and wildlife that brought visitors to the coast could take years to recover.

There is also the cost of looking after all the injured people who can no longer work. The time and effort spent coping with the dead cannot be measured. Some reports say that over 280,000 people died as a result of the tsunami. How can the long-term impact of such a number ever be truly known?

Rebuilding houses destroyed by the waves is just one of many tasks facing relief organizations.

PAYING THE PRICE

The tsunami stripped miles of beaches, seashore, and forests. The giant waves ripped through coastal forests, sand dunes, and coral **reefs**. The damage to the **environment** could last for years and leave large areas lifeless.

Millions of fish living on the coral reefs died when the giant waves washed them up on land. The coral reefs broke up or were buried under tons of mud.

A KNOCK-ON EFFECT

There are coral reefs around many of the coasts of the Indian Ocean. These look like undersea rocks but are made up of the skeletons of tiny sea creatures. Large coral reefs give shelter and food to millions of fish. Many coral reefs were destroyed by the tsunami, leaving rich fishing areas stripped. Many fishermen lost their jobs and local people no longer had a food supply. Boat builders were also out of work.

Many coral reefs were damaged by the force of the waves.

Many sea turtle eggs were washed away by the tsunami.

Mangroves are evergreen trees and shrubs. They grow on stilt-like roots in swampy areas around some coasts. Many animals live in the thick mangrove forests that protect the land against the sea and wind. In fact, the roots and branches helped to stop a lot of the tsunami's power and saved large areas of land from being swamped. But the tsunami was so powerful that many mangroves were stripped away. It may take 10 years to restore them. The full impact of the tsunami on **ecosystems** like this will probably not be known for decades.

People told stories of strange, deep-sea fish being thrown up by the tsunami on to beaches. Many were **myths**, but some large sea creatures were stranded on shore. Large sea turtles were washed up to 1.6 kilometres (1 mile) inland. They needed help to get back to the sea. The tsunami harmed these already rare animals. Many of their breeding beaches were destroyed when the sand where they lay their eggs was washed away.

THE HUMAN COST

In the Sri Lankan village of Vakarai, helpers collected people's belongings from the rubble. They put them together as a small display for survivors to visit and **mourn**. School bags, shoes, teacups, toys, and clothes were taken to a school. A label next to a shoe read, "This pair of shoes my daughter liked most."

LESSONS LEARNED

The world will be paying the price of the 2004 tsunami for many years. As the rebuilding continues, people are also working on ways to prevent similar disasters in the future. Everyone wonders when and where the next tsunami will strike, but many important lessons have been learned since 26 December 2004.

We have always known that natural disasters can affect any part of the world. In areas where tsunamis could strike, there need to be better ways of warning people that a disaster is about to happen. Relief supplies need to be ready. All countries need to plan ways of reacting to disasters. The 2004 tsunami affected more countries than other disasters. More than 50 countries were either hit by the waves or lost citizens in the areas hit.

WARNINGS

The International Tsunami Information Centre (ITIC) was set up in 1965 to warn people of possible tsunamis in the Pacific Ocean. By monitoring **sensors** in the water, sudden surges and large waves can be spotted before they reach land. Warnings can then be sent to coastguards and the media, although usually only a couple of hours' warning can be given.

Satellite photos can show if a tsunami is about to strike.

Coastal zones and small islands are often **densely populated**. This increases the risk. Nearly 3 billion people (almost half the world's population) live near the sea. As sea levels keep rising in many parts of the world, more work will need to be done to protect coastal areas from the power of the sea.

Knowing more about tsunamis will help to protect people in the future. In Thailand more than 1,800 people were saved because a tribal chief noticed that the sea was moving differently. He recognised there was something wrong and decided to **evacuate** his people to the hills. When people are aware of what can happen, they are more likely to respond and survive.

When people know that a tsunami is on its way, there is no doubt that lives can be saved. By the time the 2004 tsunami reached Africa, many people on Kenya's coast had been warned so they could escape in time.

There is now a real need for countries around the Indian Ocean to develop an early warning system so that they are ready next time. It can only be a matter of time before another underwater earthquake strikes.

This warning **buoy** can warn people on land of an approaching tsunami.

The United States use high-tech buoys to sense an approaching tsunami. From mid 2007, this DART programme (Deep-ocean Assessment and Reporting of Tsunami) should be warning if a tsunami is on its way to US coasts. Maybe all coasts round the world will soon be able to afford the cost of such technology. Only then will many lives be saved if disaster strikes once more.

TIMELINE

Sunday 26 December 2004:
12:59 a.m. GMT (7:59 a.m. local time):

An earthquake measuring 9 on the Richter scale is recorded off the coast of Sumatra, Indonesia. Buildings shake in Bangkok, Thailand, around 1,260 kilometres (780 miles) away as well as in Singapore, 950 kilometres (590 miles away). Several strong **aftershocks** follow.

1:30 a.m. GMT (8:30 a.m. local time):

The first waves strike Sumatra in Indonesia.

2:30 a.m. GMT (9:30 a.m. local time):

The waves reach Thailand.

3:00 a.m. GMT (9:00 a.m. local time):

Southern India and Sri Lanka are hit by the waves.

4:30 a.m. GMT (9:30 a.m. local time):

The Maldives are flooded by the tsunami.

5:12 a.m. GMT (11:12 a.m. local time):

150 people are reported dead in Sri Lanka. Within 30 minutes, the figure reaches 3,000.

7:00 to 8:00 a.m. GMT (10:00 to 11:00 a.m. local time):

The waves reach East Africa.

Monday 27 December:

A massive rescue operation begins. The estimated death toll reaches 26,000, with at least 12,000 in Sri Lanka alone.

Tuesday 28 December:

> The death toll rises to 60,000. Mass burials of bodies begin.

Wednesday 29 December:

> The death toll is predicted to exceed 100,000. The confirmed figure rises to 77,000.

Thursday 30 December:

> The death toll approaches 120,000.

Friday 31 December:

> The United Nations warns the tsunami death toll could reach 150,000.

19 January 2005:

> The death toll in Indonesia alone nearly doubles to more than 166,000. This is later revised to about 130,000. Media reports say worldwide deaths stand at more than 250,000.

26 December 2005:

> Millions of people take part in ceremonies to mark the first anniversary of the disaster.

GLOSSARY

aftershock smaller earth tremors that often follow a major earthquake

aid providing help to disaster victims, such as supplies and medical support

buoy floating object anchored in water as a marker or to warn of danger

capsize turn over

cholera disease giving severe vomiting and diarrhea. It is caused by bacteria and can be fatal.

contaminate make impure or unfit for use

counselling advice and emotional support

criticism careful judgement

crust outer part of Earth. Earth's crust is made of solid rock and is between 10 and 50 kilometres (6 and 30 miles) thick.

debris remains of something broken down or destroyed

densely populated large number of people living very closely together

desperation loss of hope and feeling of misery or dread

devastation complete ruin

ecosystem balance between living things interacting with their natural environment

environment surrounding conditions, such as soil and plants that affect survival of life

epicentre point on the Earth's surface directly above the focus of an earthquake

evacuate remove people from a place of danger

GMT Greenwich Mean Time

horizon line in the distance where the ground or sea seems to meet the sky

malaria disease caught from the bite of mosquitoes, causing fever and even death

mangrove tropical tree or shrub growing dense roots in salty marsh or shallow water

mosque Muslim place of worship

mourn feel or show grief or sorrow over someone's death

myth popular belief that is false or not entirely real

orphaned be left without any parents when they both die

plate huge moving piece of Earth's crust

reef chain of rocks or ridge of sand at or near the surface of water

remote far away from any towns

Richter scale scale used to show the strength of an earthquake

sensor device that detects movement and responds by transmitting a signal

stagnant very still

torrent violent stream of liquid, flowing at great force

trauma serious reaction to severe mental or emotional stress or injury

UNICEF United Nations Children's Fund

United Nations worldwide organization of countries, begun in 1945

vibration trembling motion

FINDING OUT MORE

BOOKS

Defining Moments: Disasters, Sandra Forty (Thunder Bay, 2006)

The Raging Sea: The Powerful Account of the Worst Tsunami in U.S. History, Dennis M. Powers (Citadel, 2005)

Tsunami Diary, John Townsend (Hodder Murray, 2006)

Tsunami: Hope, Heroes and Incredible Stories of Survival, Joe Funk (Triumph, 2005)

Tsunami Man: Learning About Killer Waves with Walter Dudley, Anthony D. Fredericks (University of Hawaii Press, 2002)

Tsunami: The World's Most Terrifying Natural Disaster, Geoff Tibballs (Carlton Books, 2005)

Turbulent Planet: Wild Water: Floods, Tony Allan (Raintree, 2004)

Waves: From Surfing to Tsunami, Drew Kampion (Gibbs Smith, 2005)

WEBSITES

www.nationalgeographic.com/ngkids/9610/kwave
This website contains animations showing how tsunamis form and spread around the world, plus the story of a tsunami survivor.

earthquake.usgs.gov/4kids
This website is full of facts and information about why earthquakes happen. You can also find out about the latest earthquakes to have struck around the world.